MY PLACE IN HISTORY

# My Life in a CHINOOK VILLAGE

By Max Caswell

Gareth Stevens
PUBLISHING

**Please visit our website, www.garethstevens.com. For a free color catalog of all our high-quality books, call toll free 1-800-542-2595 or fax 1-877-542-2596.**

**Library of Congress Cataloging-in-Publication Data**

Names: Caswell, Max, author.
Title: My life in a Chinook village / Max Caswell.
Description: New York : Gareth Stevens Publishing, [2018] | Series: My place in history | Includes index.
Identifiers: LCCN 2017010329| ISBN 9781538203019 (pbk. book) | ISBN 9781538203026 (6 pack) | ISBN 9781538203033 (library bound book)
Subjects: LCSH: Chinook Indians–History–Juvenile literature. | Chinook Indians–Social life and customs–Juvenile literature.
Classification: LCC E99.C57 C37 2018 | DDC 979.5004/9741–dc23
LC record available at https://lccn.loc.gov/2017010329

Published in 2018 by
**Gareth Stevens Publishing**
111 East 14th Street, Suite 349
New York, NY 10003



Designer: Bethany Perl
Editor: Joan Stoltman

Photo credits: Cover, p. 1 A. T. Agate, R. W. Dawson/courtesy of the Library of Congress; cover, p. 1 (background) Natalia Sheinkin/Shutterstock.com; cover, pp. 1–24 (torn strip) barbaliss/Shutterstock.com; cover, pp. 1–24 (photo frame) Davor Ratkovic/Shutterstock.com; cover, pp. 1–24 (white paper) HABRDA/Shutterstock.com; cover, pp. 1–24 (parchment) M. Unal Ozmen/Shutterstock.com; cover, pp. 1–24 (textured edge) saki80/Shutterstock.com; pp. 1–24 (paper background) Kostenko Maxim/Shutterstock.com; p. 5 Luchenko Yana/Shutterstock.com; p. 7 Walter Siegmund/Wikipedia.org; p. 9 (wapato plant) born1945/flickr.com; p. 9 (wapato bulb) Wikipedia.org; p. 11 (inset) courtesy of the Library of Congress; pp. 11 (main image), 15 (spear fisherman) Edward S. Curtis/courtesy of the Library of Congress; p. 13 Seth Eastman/Archive Photos/Getty Images; pp. 15 (fishing net), 17, 19 Buyenlarge/Archive Photos/Getty Images; p. 21 (basket) courtesy of the Smithsonian Institution; p. 21 (waterfall) Frederica Grassi/Moment Open/Getty Images.



Printed in the United States of America

CPSIA compliance information: Batch #CS17GS: For further information contact Gareth Stevens, New York, New York at 1-800-542-2595.

# CONTENTS



Words in the glossary appear in **bold** type the first time they are used in the text.

# Born to TRADE

October 7, 1779

My older brothers all fish for salmon like my father. But when I was born, Grandfather said an elk spirit told him I would become a great trader. Trading is a **tradition** that our people, and my grandfather, are well known for.

Grandfather made me this cedar journal to practice my language skills to prepare for being a trader. He wrapped it in elk hide he traded for just for me! I hope I can live up to Grandfather and the elk spirit's **expectations**.

## Notes from History

A young Chinook child wouldn't have known English, but rather Chinook. The language isn't spoken by anyone today.

"Chinook" refers to 30 different Native American groups who all spoke the same language, Chinook. They lived along the Columbia River—*Yakaitl-Wimakl* in Chinook—as well as the Willamette and the Clackamas Rivers in what are now Washington and Oregon.

# Our WINTER HOME

November 6, 1779

Now that it's cold, we're in our big house. Ours has a salmon totem pole carved by my uncle to keep us safe. My mother's whole family lives under this roof during winter—all 50 of us! We live in the back next to Mother's parents.

This winter, Father and my brothers are mending their fishing baskets, and Grandfather is preparing beaver hides for trade. Mother keeps very busy making food, but she has time to play "roll the dice" with her sisters, too.

## Notes from History

**Chinook winter villages—built in the forest, away from the shore—could have as many as 35 plank houses. Plank houses could be large enough to house 100 people and were made from giant red cedar trees.**

In a Chinook plank house, each family had their own room along the outer walls, separated from each other by hanging hides or blankets. A large central fire pit was used for cooking, eating, and storytelling.

# STORYTELLING

December 20, 1779

In winter, we eat the smoke-dried meats and fish that my aunts prepared all summer long. Mother dried some berries for a special winter treat. We eat the **camas** and **wapato** dug up in summer, too. There's nothing like roasted wapato on a cold day!

Every night, we all gather around the fire to hear stories. For now, I listen—but I'm working on a story of my own. I know that **trickster** Blue-Jay will be in it!

### Notes from History

Blue-Jay is the hero of many funny Chinook stories. He is very foolish, so his plans go off track. His sister, Ioi, always tries to help, but she usually suffers.

The Chinook people taught, **entertained** each other, and passed down their **religion** through storytelling. In their religion, animals and things in nature all had spirits and powers.

# RAIN, RAIN, RAIN

January 22, 1780

Today, it's so cold I had to wear a deer-hide robe! Usually, our winters are more wet than cold.

Last summer, our village took down two mighty red cedar trees. We use cedar bark to make everything—from rope and rain hats to **cloaks** and kitchen supplies. Did you know cedar clothing keeps you totally dry? Now that it's winter, my father's brothers set to work cutting each trunk into a 15-person canoe. They're canoe makers, but I don't know how they do it!

*Notes from History*

To make a tree trunk into a canoe, the Chinook first burned and then cut away wood to form a canoe shape. Then, they'd soften the wood with steam, boiling water, and hot rocks to stretch and shape it.

CHINOOK CANOE

The Chinook people made six different kinds of canoes. Each tree was chosen carefully, and canoes were treated with great care. They believed a canoe held the tree's spirit and honoring the spirit kept them safe on the water.

# MOVING

March 17, 1780

It's finally warm enough to head to *Yakaitl-Wimakl*! I'm looking forward to working on my shell necklace. I only need five or six more shells! Hopefully, I'll have it done in time for the first-salmon feast!

My brothers are working on our summer cedar-bark homes, but I get to run and play! Last year, they said I was too young to play the laughing game, but now I'm 8, so they better let me!

## Notes from History

In the laughing game, sticks are placed between two groups. The goal is to get the most sticks. You each take a turn trying to grab a stick, but you can't grab a stick while laughing—and the other team's trying to make you laugh!

Chinook children and men loved spending time in the warm months playing sports. The Chinook, the Sioux—who are in this painting—and many other native groups often played a game a lot like modern lacrosse.

# FISHING

April 12, 1780

My brothers are excited to fish again! They get very bored in the winter when they can't do their job.

Last year, Father tried fishing with a net and liked it, so this year, they'll use spears, Father's net, and maybe even a basket! Mother and her sisters are in charge of smoking the fish. They smoke large amounts for our winter supply and for Grandfather to trade. If only the salmon would just get here already!

### Notes from History

In Chinook culture, each fishing area was controlled by a certain family. Families traded throughout the summer to get fish from areas run by other families, including those in other villages.

Plants and trees—like nettle, rush, willow bark, and cedar—provided the fibers used to make fishing nets and baskets.

# *First* SALMON

June 29, 1780

The salmon have returned! My family's going to be very busy, as Father is salmon chief this year!

This morning at the first-salmon **ceremony**, Father led the village in thanking the salmon king for allowing the salmon to give themselves to our village again this year. He chose Mother's brother to catch the first salmon later today. Both men will get their ears **pierced** tonight to record this important day. Then, Father will let the salmon swim past for 3 days.

### *Notes from History*

The Chinook people believed that salmon had spirits that lived forever. The salmon king would order them to feed the Chinook people every June. Then their spirits returned to the water.

Even today, from the moment it's caught to the moment its bones are placed back in the river, the first salmon's head must point upriver so that its spirit knows how to get home.

# Our Family's POTLATCH

July 1, 1780

We've danced and sung for days and had the first-salmon feast. Tonight, our family hosts a potlatch. We've sent messengers by canoe to invite our neighbors to the event. When they arrive tonight, each village will dance. Then our family will give them furs, salmon, necklaces, and other presents.

Our faces painted, we'll wear our finest beads and shells and furs tonight. I'll wear an otter fur that Grandfather passed down to me when I was born and the shell necklace that I just finished!

### Notes from History

A potlatch is a celebration, or party, that lasts many days and is held whenever someone is born, died, or married, in addition to other major life events.

A family saved and traded for years to be able give away gifts when hosting a potlatch. The more a family gave away, the more honor they received. Potlatches were held often, so people would get their gifts back.

# *packing for* THE DALLES

August 1, 1780

I'm helping Grandfather pack for his yearly trading journey to the Dalles waterfall. Our people are known there for our smoked salmon. Grandfather will bring three different kinds of salmon—sockeye, pink, and, of course, Chinook—that we've gotten through fishing and local trade, so he'll be very popular!

Grandfather will also be bringing four canoes for trading, as well as some baskets, a few furs, and some horn carvings. I can't wait to see what he returns with!

## *Notes from History*

**Because the Chinook people controlled trade on the Columbia River, they controlled all trade along the West Coast, including everything that moved east to the Dalles along the Columbia River.**

Once a year for thousands of years, a great trade fair happened at the Dalles waterfall. It was the largest trade fair in western North America, and the Chinook people were a major part of it.

CHINOOK BASKET

# GLOSSARY

**camas:** a bulb related to lily flowers that grows in meadows and is baked for food

**ceremony:** an event to honor or celebrate something

**cloak:** a kind of coat that has no sleeves and is worn over the shoulders and joined at the neck

**entertain:** to do things that are interesting for people to watch or listen to

**expectation:** a belief that something will happen or is likely to happen

**pierce:** to make a hole through

**religion:** a belief in and way of honoring a god or gods

**tradition:** a long-practiced way of life

**trickster:** one who tricks or deceives people, especially in order to get something

**wapato:** a bulb about the size of a chicken's egg that grows in the wetlands and can be roasted or boiled for food

# For more INFORMATION

## Books

Cohen, Fiona. *Curious Kids Nature Guide: Explore the Amazing Outdoors of the Pacific Northwest.* Seattle, WA: Little Bigfoot, 2017.

Goddu, Krystyna Poray. *Native Peoples of the Northwest.* Minneapolis, MN: Lerner Publications, 2017.

Sonneborn, Liz. *Northwest Coast Indians.* Chicago, IL: Heinemann Library, 2012.

## Websites

**Chinook Nation for Kids**

*mrnussbaum.com/nativeamericans/chinook/*

This website digs into four parts of Chinook lifestyle: diet, home, culture, and potlatch.

**Chinook Tribe**

*warpaths2peacepipes.com/indian-tribes/chinook-tribe.htm*

Read all sorts of interesting information about the Chinook people.

**Publisher's note to educators and parents:** Our editors have carefully reviewed these websites to ensure that they are suitable for students. Many websites change frequently, however, and we cannot guarantee that a site's future contents will continue to meet our high standards of quality and educational value. Be advised that students should be closely supervised whenever they access the Internet.

# INDEX